The World Outside My Window

By

Dan Hanosh

© 2004 by Dan Hanosh. All rights reserved.

No part of this book may be reproduced, stored in a retrieval system, or transmitted by any means, electronic, mechanical, photocopying, recording, or otherwise, without written permission from the author.

First published by AuthorHouse 06/08/04

ISBN: 1-4184-6860-6 (e-book)
ISBN: 1-4184-3538-4 (Paperback)

This book is printed on acid free paper.

"Cardinals Call", first published in Love and Laughter by The International Library of Poetry.

"Caught in a Breeze", first published in Theatre of The Mind by Nobel House Publishers.

"I Will", first published in the Kiwanews, June 2003.

"The Painting", first published in The Best Poems & Poets of 2002 by The International Library of Poetry.

This book is dedicated to Doris Hanosh, my beloved mother. She taught me to reach for my dreams. Now that she is gone, each day I go on writing, thinking of her with each word, each poem that I write. Thank you mom, I will not quit.

For Dad, times have been hard. Thank you.

For Deb, Pam and Chris, thanks for your support.

Thank you Sue, Robert and Jordan, All my love, always.

Growing up my report cards always held the same message, he's spending too much time day dreaming, now my message to all is, Dreams are yours to share.

Change starts with each of us.

To everyone who has supported my effort, thank you.

Table of Contents

For Those I Leave Behind.............. 1
The World Outside My Window........... 3
Writing............................... 6
How Can I Ever Trust Again............ 7
Chris................................. 9
One Day a Year........................ 10
A Teardrop............................ 12
Dream Traveler........................ 13
A Gesture............................. 14
Minnehaha............................. 16
Divided Once More..................... 19
I Will................................ 23
The Cold Has Come Again............... 24
Winter Snow........................... 25
Snowflake Warriors.................... 27
Cardinals Call........................ 28
The Fox............................... 29
It could happen....................... 32
Nothing Ever Changes.................. 33
Caught in a Breeze.................... 36
The Dock.............................. 37
Big Sky............................... 42
The Ruby.............................. 43

The American Eagle	46
The Finals	49
I am still free	51
Life	53
Full Circle	54
The House on Orchard	55
The Storm	57
Tending the Garden	59
Stormy Day	61
Slot Fever	63
Loved From Afar	67
Blue Skies	70
The Reason I Live	72
Together, Again	74
The Painting	76
Growing Old	78
Today I Start a Journey	79
The Distraction	80
Losing My Convictions	84
How Did This Happen?	85
Columbia, where are you?	88
Danny's Sign of Spring moved me so	89
My Secret Place	91
Star Lake	94
My Last Moments at the Lake	96
Alone	99

My Neurosis	101
I wonder where	103
Foot Steps Echo in the Night	104
A Taste of Freedom	106
The Canyon of My Youth	109
The Special People	111
Gone Forever	112
A Chill	113
My Way	115
My World	116
The Major	117
I Remember	119
Canada	120
His Day	125
Today we travel a familiar path,	127
Graduation Day	129
FOR I AM AN AMERICAN	131
The Righteous War	133
Only Suffering	134
War is still War	136
Everlasting Peace	138
Fail them, not	141
The Plant	143
This Cage We Call Life	146
By Beginning	151
What is Fiction	153

The Writing Stopped	155
A Pencil Poised	157
My Ghost, the Writer	158
A Poet	160
Two Lives	162
Summer of my youth	164
A Portrait of a Man	166
Be Proud, Jennifer	167
The Rodeo	169
Spring	170
Choices	172
Thank You Son	174
My Choice	177
Protesting War	179
Outside My Window	181
Time	182
Life, A Game	183
The Last Story	184
Emotional Me	186

For Those I Leave Behind

(for Sue)

Yesterday,
the leaves were green,
today,
yellows, browns and reds,
are all that can
be seen,

falling,
from lofty perches,
another
summer has come and gone,
another ring around my trunk,
as the year winds down,

closer
to the end,
then

to where it all began,

those, many years,

long ago,

staring

through the window, I see myself,

wondering,

if I've made a difference,

for those I

leave behind?

The World Outside My Window

Through the trees, opaque
billowy pillows, splash on
an azure canvas, sailing furiously,
beyond my view.

Trees bending, each limb,
each branch, separately
shifting, everything dusted,
by a cold white blanket.

The hard rust road,
emitting bits, pieces,
translucent, behind the gray
dismal trees, now empty.

A picture, its beauty, a mere
landscape, unknown to all,

framed by my window where I work,
each day, composing, my words.

The sun breaks, the silence,
momentarily, revealing itself,
another frothy foam drowning
the expressions of light.

The green needles of a lone pine,
dangle, high above, scooping up
the rays of the sun,
today, there are few.

Sounds of motion, rush by,
swoosh, invading
my senses, suggesting
movement, contour.

Another cloud seizes the
sun, insinuating what

will surely come,
maybe not today, but soon.

Cold, moisture falling,
again, from the sky,
clouds, delivering white starlets,
multifaceted inhabitants.

Cumulus, like trees, dropping
their unneeded luggage,
as though aging, as a man
losing his youth.

Today, I understand,
the world outside
my window, a fragile old world,
that's getting older.

Writing

The words,
must be
recorded,

they don't
have to be right,
not right away,

changes solve
the problems, though they
must flow and

continue,
until they fill
the page,

a chapter, a
novel, and much,
much, more.

How Can I Ever Trust Again

Tears come late at
night, I sense
your pain,

from deep within,
somehow, we are
to blame,

betrayal stings,

your not alone,
you need to know,
we're here,

one day, you have
to forgive, to
forget,

you should move on,

trust is a must,
for finding,
friendship,

you ask, how can
I ever trust
again,

still, you have to.

Chris

You're a special person,
chosen for some
unknown reason.

Once an energetic youth,
slowly, debilitated, still
you keep a positive outlook.

I knew you when
you were a child,
I bounced you on my knee.

I know you as a young adult,
together we write
of your dreams.

The hardships you have endured,
have made you wise
beyond your years,

Today, I write for you,
I'm proud to call you,
My Friend.

One Day a Year

My first time,
I wasn't sure I
could do it, I
blanked my mind,
raised my gloved
hand, the one that
held the axe,

I told myself
that's why I
raise them, that's
what everyone
did, at one time,

my nerves were jumpy,
my eye was sure,
my arm dropped
as did the axe,

a few flaps, and that
bird was no more,

I never liked killing,
takes me weeks to
build the nerve and
just as long to forget,
still, one day a year, I
become my father's father,
remembering, how
life used to be.

A Teardrop

A teardrop falls
from a child's eye
hitting the ground,
shattering,
scattering,
everywhere,
becoming a stream,
a river,
an ocean.
A hand waves
from a neighbor's hand
inciting a wave
smiling,
laughing,
everywhere,
becoming a friend,
a family,
a nation.

Dream Traveler

I'm on a journey, beside a stream,
every step brings me closer to my dream,
although, my destiny has become blurred,
as if it blended into that opaque sky,
confused, I stop and wonder why,
for tomorrow, seems nearer
while the burden maybe dearer
yet, a fork in my path,
brings doubt into my math,
fear, I might choose wrong,
should I stop, go back or go on.

A Gesture

Today, I was moved,
touched, not by any earth
rocking event, but a
gesture, so small and yet
large enough that it reached
deep into my soul.

Today, I went for a drive,
my thoughts wandering, as everything
flew by, remembering the good times,
I missed her smile, her laugh and
those oh, so special hugs.

This day driving, tears running,
someone reached out to me, at a tollbooth,
the operator waved me on, someone
had paid for me, someone had seen my pain,
then I realized, it didn't matter.

Today, at that moment I knew,
a stranger had reached out, had felt my pain,
it was my turn, to stop the pity,
to pass on a gesture, to someone
who needed it, more than I.

For the first time, I realized, actions alone
will change the world, making it a better place,
just one small gesture, simply someone
reaching out, showed me, that
I was loved, and now, I reach out to you,
for you to are loved.

Minnehaha

Past the town of North Prairie,
through the berg of Eagle, route N
and into the parking lot.

Walking alone, along the smooth blacktop path,
I'm transported to a time, one
of less stress.

The down trodden snow speaks
the message of those who've
come before me.

Nature's beauty abounds,
in a snow covered pine tree, in the
chirping of an occasional bird.

The air is silent, with it's
tone of peace, the message
for the day.

Each step reminds me of what was, left
by those that came before, many who also
cherished the waters of the spring.

Musical sounds fill the silence,
the strumming as the water exits the shambles
of the springhouse,

the drumming, as it falls onto
the rocks below, vibrations,
music for all.

Memories of what man has created,
stands erect, still marking
the shores of the pond.

Visitors drink it's waters,
fish from her banks, wade into
the depths.

Tranquility draws them back,
time after time,
touched by the beauty.

Fly fisherman fish
for the trout that live
in it's safety.

This is a place of building, a positive,
to reinforce ones own existence,
a place of healing.

The spring is my spiritual retreat, bound
through the reading of a poem or the simple act
of creating, a thought, worthy of writing.

Many know it as Paradise Springs, but for me
it will always be Minnehaha, my Garden of Eden,
my utopian dream and my salvation.

Divided Once More

Split,
divided among
individual
ideals,

not since
the great war
have we been so
pulled apart,

our values
have been
sacrificed for
a cause,

righteous,
maybe once,
preemptive force
has never been our way,

at least, until
now, policy gone
astray, the arrogance
of man,

fear
has captured
America, has
taken hold,

changed
our values,
stole our
freedoms

and
still,
we are not
secure,

split,

are our

rights,

taken away,

and

still

the dying

goes on,

we tried

force,

to create

a democracy

and

we don't

know why

we fail,

now,

we are

divided

once more.

I Will

be there when
I'm called to serve,
not always sure how,
not always as chipper
as I should, but
I will be there.

I will be there,
trying to build
a better tomorrow,
to be a better
friend, to
strengthen what
binds us
together.

I will be there
to ring bells,
sell candy or paint.
If we pledge to help
count on me,
I will be
there.

The Cold Has Come Again

Gazing out,
through my window,
barren gray trees
stand, tall against
the deep blue, of a
cold winter's sky,

brown leaves, lay
asleep, on the forest floor,
a lonely pine, shows it's
green branches, vividly,
against the dismal
grays and browns,

the green grass,
now brown, squirrel nests, no
longer hidden in the trees,
nothing moving, the geese have
gone, gone till spring, for
the cold has come again.

Winter Snow

Bits

pieces

pounding

within

a cloud.

Shaped

contours

collecting

cold

as ice.

White

fluff

falling

from

above.

Ice
crystals
crowding
against
the door.

Tiny
flakes
fleeing
over
driveways.

Winter
snow
shackling
my
spirit.

Snowflake Warriors

Colors
fly,
governing,
flakes fall,
appearing similar,
yet so very

different.

Slowly,
they wage
a battle, starting
with a small insertion,
dropping, gathering on the
ground, before the chaos of

the major offensive.

Warriors
drop through
the clouds, in numbers
too high to count, falling
to their end, their demise,
landing, to be shoveled into
a pile, forgotten, forever.

Cardinals Call

(For Matthew)

Root rue, Root rue,
   Sings the Cardinal,
     As everyone rises
To begin the day.

Friends Everywhere,
   Friends Everywhere,
     Only if we acknowledge
What they say.

Understanding the message,
   Is no easy task,
     We analyze, evaluate and interpret,
Can it be?

The message is unique,
   To each,
     Imagination,
Is the key.

The Fox

One night, my boy found
a baby fox, running,
through the neighborhood.

Why did my boy, try to catch it.

It's mother,
high-tailed for the kit,
rescuing it.

Last night,
it rained, a heavy
down poor rain.

Walking, I found a
baby fox,
it lay still,

Oh, so water logged,

it must have
drowned.

Sadness,
entered my thoughts,
I stood, wondering, why.

Why do the innocent, have to die?

Months before,
a neighbor girl, stood
there for the bus,

she waited and was hit
by a car,
she died.

Sadness,
entered my thoughts,
I stood, wondering, why.

Why do the innocent, have to die?

Why the baby

fox, why had it fallen,

near my driveway?

Did the mother

leave it, knowing I

respected it

or did she kill the kit,

blaming my

son for it.

I dug a hole, prayed,

for them both,

may they rest.

Sadness,

entered my thoughts,

I stood, wondering, why.

Why do the innocent, have to die?

It could happen

High from above
well into the sky
fly birds with very
large wings.

No one has ever admitted
to seeing them, not anymore,
at least not for a
hundred years.

Not until the
little boy went missing,
did anyone suspect,
a bird.

Folk lore hints of them,
birds so big they can carry
away a person as large as
a man.

It happens all the time,
attacks from the sky, people always
pointing their weapons high, toward
the heavens, always ready.

With a cry, they swoop in,
grabbing a victim in their talons,
pulling them into the blueness,

taking them away, forever.

Nothing Ever Changes

Entering the dark room,
Cotton white sheets on the bed,
Paint caked windows,
Gloomy tile lain on the floor,
Nurses wearing knee length dresses,
Caps on their heads, not
A sound except the moaning, from
Out in the hall, hand crank
Beds, steel chairs line the wall,
Antiseptic aroma in the air,
And the people, slowly, dying.

Things always seem to change,
Never really remain the same,
Time has no conscience,
Everyone's lost in their own pain,
Babies breathe life,
Youth build hope,

Elders fight for their rights,
And the dying pray for death,
Nothing ever changes,
Nothing ever changes,
Nothing ever changes, anymore.

Entering the white dark room,
Paper sheets on the bed,
Paint clad metal windows,
Bright linoleum lain on the floor,
Nurse's brightly colored pants suits,
No caps on their heads,
Sounds from a TV, blaring, across the hall,
Electronic gauges on the bed,
Cloth chair against the wall,
No aroma in the air,
And the people, slowly, dying.

Things always seem to change,
Never really remain the same,
Time has no conscience,

Everyone's lost in their own pain,
Babies breathe life,
Youth build hope,
Elders fight for their rights,
And the dying pray for death,
Nothing ever changes,
Nothing ever changes,
Nothing ever changes, anymore.

Caught in a Breeze

Grains of sand,
sift, through
my fingers,

Falling, for a moment,
tiny particles, adrift,
toward the ground,

Instantly, their
destiny, becomes a thing
of chance,

Caught in a breeze,
some spread their wings,
achieving, new heights,

The rest, slowly,
falling, to be with
the others.

The Dock

(For Mom)

Discontent finally forced me to change my life,
my time on earth had been wasted, I looked for contentment
where I was happiest, doing what made me happy, I went
north fishing.

> *Something is wrong I sense it,*
> *No one talks about it, though it is there,*
> *She doesn't sleep nights through anymore,*
> *No one thinks this is unusual,*
> *but me,…I say nothing..*

Three years searching, to find what was missing, my career
hadn't satisfied me, I longed for more, so I started to
paint, still, I needed more, I took up fly fishing, I
read to learn, causing me to remember my love of reading,
learning, I wrote several friends, their letters enraged my
senses, a new energy filled me. Why, I thought?

> *Something is wrong I sense it,*
> *No one talks about it, though it is there,*
> *She doesn't sleep nights through anymore,*
> *No one thinks this is unusual,*
> *but me,…I say nothing..*

To write, to preserve, just an idea, but wasn't that what my career was all about, ideas, though, they were not saved, not written, therefore not valued. If what I create is not kept, did that mean, my life had no worth? I'm not sure, although, I knew I had found, my destiny, I must write.

> *Something is wrong I sense it,*
> *No one talks about it, though it is there,*
> *She doesn't sleep nights through anymore,*
> *No one thinks this is unusual,*
> *but me,…I say nothing..*

She was my friend, my confidant, I'm not sure she approved of my writing, although, she didn't let on, for that was her way, we talked everyday, many thought, I should work a regular job, give up writing, but for me, to write is to live and I go on,

> *Something is wrong I sense it,*
> *No one talks about it, though it is there,*
> *She doesn't sleep nights through anymore,*
> *No one thinks this is unusual,*
> *but me,…I say nothing..*

Weekends, I would go north to see them both, writing gave me my freedom to take the trips, I needed experiences to write about, field research, I called them, we would go to fish fry on Friday nights, later to the casino. How she loved the casino.

> *Something is wrong I sense it,*
> *No one talks about it, though it is there,*
> *She doesn't sleep nights through anymore,*
> *No one thinks this is unusual,*
> *but me,…I say nothing..*

After dinner once, we went fishing off a dock, spending hours, pulling in small bluegills, she caught more than any of us, always, we went to the casino, Dad was concerned, each morning he was having to wake her.

> *Something is wrong I sense it,*
> *No one talks about it, though it is there,*
> *She doesn't sleep nights through anymore,*
> *No one thinks this is unusual,*
> *but me,...I say nothing..*

I was very busy writing stories, I still I talked to her every other day, when she became short of breath, I told her to go to the doctor, pneumonia is what they said, I hoped so, although, down deep, I thought differently.

> *Something is wrong I sense it,*
> *No one talks about it, though it is there,*
> *She doesn't sleep nights through anymore,*
> *No one thinks this is unusual,*
> *but me,...I say nothing..*

Now she is gone, I miss her greatly, she was my motivation, my confidant and my friend, now, she is with me, in my heart and in my memories, everytime I write, I think of her, telling myself each day, I will not quit, I will not fail… I write on, for her.

> *Something is wrong I sense it,*
> *No one talks about it, though it is there,*
> *She doesn't sleep nights through anymore,*
> *No one thinks this is unusual,*
> *but me,…I say nothing..*

Big Sky

Looking around,
I quickly realize,
why I'm drawn
back each year,
to this place,
Montana.

In the distance,
a mountain can be seen,
with it's browns, grays and
greens, sun shining bright,
overhead, a turquoise backdrop
and white puffy clouds.

Farther, in the distance,
another mountain and still another,
all against the blue background of the sky,
with it's opaque, billowy clouds,
big sky, like one would see,
in a magazine.

The Ruby

Off the beaten path,
away from the busy highways,
strangers come as
always,

the river meanders
through the countryside,
winding, just a mere
stream,

once the clinking of
pans, echoed through the
valley, sounds of forty-niners,
seeking gold, garnets,

now, the plopping
of fishermen treading
through its waters,
along its bank's,

imitation flies softly caress
its surface, tempting
large browns, to rise,
to bite,

shale piles creep along its edges,
left long ago, the towns
are gone, away, the buildings
are no more,

snakes slithering through
the shale piles, trout hiding
beneath its waters, in the cool
ripples, clear as a summer day,

buzzing flies, biting,
stinging areas
of an arm, a leg,
a neck,

a lone trout rises with

a swirl, catching

a dun, a caddis, awakening,

the Ruby, once more.

The American Eagle

The anticipation soared as we waited. People in front of us, people behind us. We could not move without bumping someone. Sweat ran down my neck. Cries of excitement filled the air.

Then we moved forward.

We were herded together like cattle, weaving this way and that. Bars contained us; chains blocked the avenues of possible escape. Clanging could be heard in the background, metal hitting metal.

Then we moved forward.

Time was moving so slowly. We talked among ourselves, about everything and nothing. Everyone was watching the animated characters on the viewing screens to pass the time. Girls giggled, boys acted tough, kids were restless. All anxious, anxiously waiting.

Then we moved forward.

Now, we reached the gate. Whoosh, the car moved, in we climbed. Bars pinning us in, holding us. We dared not move. Off our car went, out of the shoot, out on our own, alone.

Then we moved forward.

Up, Up we went. Click, click, click, we climbed the white wooden structure. We could see forever. The trees seemed like small bushes. Our car in the parking lot, no bigger than a dot. My mind raced, realizing my mortality.

Then we moved forward.

Jerkingly, we reached the top. Just a moment, time stood still. Epiphany, climax, culmination. Down, down the car sped, everyone screaming. Some waving they're arms, enjoying the thrill, others eyes closed, holding on tightly, seeing their life pass before them, in horror.

Then we moved forward.

Now, we're out of control, nothing anyone could do. We were in God's hands. Would it ever end? ... The car looped once, then twice, up we went again to the top. Down, quickly, sharply, banking to the right, then the left. Surely, the steel could not hold. Everyone screaming.

Then we moved forward.

To the right, then the left the car was slowing. Suddenly, jerking to a screeching halt, then continuing ever so slowly to the gate. Finally the car stopped, we climbed, quickly out. Leaving the gate, everyone talking, let's do it again. We have to go again.

Then we moved forward.

The Finals

Competitors,
everyone of them,
one must win,
the other will lose,
although just walking onto
the court, distinguishes each
from all others,
no shame tonight,
only the spoils,
in the contest
to the best.

Ten
players, battling,
for the top
honors, five attacking,
five defending,
the ball, speedily,

travels the court
and into the hoop,
again, hurrying to
the other end,
a shot,
swish.

Each
possession, a war,
every basket
a victory, yet
when the clock
reaches zero, only
one will be in
the lead and
the other, down
by just
three.

I am still free

A symbol, sits in
front of me,
a token of freedom,
each day, I see it,
shinny, ominous, surrounded
by trivial nick-knacks,
just knowing,
it's there,
reassures me.

Everyone, plans
for retirement,
I live for today,
enjoying my journey,
enjoying the path,
growing old seems so harsh,
remembering, the jokes,
the old people,

relief, sits before me,
allowing peace to enter
my thoughts, I will
not be a burden,
I will not become
an non-entity.

When the
time is right,
I am not sure,
I will act,
but today,
it reminds me,
I am still
free, still able
to control
my destiny.

Life

The Light
      Comes on
           An idea is formed.

To Act
      Or not to act
           A choice is made.

The Light
      Goes off
           All is lost, forever.

Full Circle

Sides are being chosen,
    Groups are gathering in the night,
        Divide and conquer,
            Is their call.

Taxes, Taxes, Taxes,
    For this or for that,
        Everyone, unaware
            What truly is important.

Politicians, know our wants,
    They say, they will never hurt us,
        Make us pay, for what
            We do not want.

Taxes, Taxes, Taxes,
    Revolt is the cry,
        For we, will not pay, the tax
            On their TEA.

The House on Orchard

I bought a vacant house on Orchard,
all the windows on the porch were broken,
the owner, they say, she had Alzheimer's disease.

Each day, I worked on the house, I began to know her well,
with each room's color, the curtains covering the
windowsills, I often imagined her sitting, at the table,
where she paid her bills.

Her path, was worn on the carpeted steps, that led to the
second floor, she must of climbed them, hundreds of times,
past the built in dresser, down the long dark hall, to the
yellow bedroom.

Everywhere, was her touch, every room, contained a trace,
she left behind, termites shared the basement, the garage
was falling down and yet the house was still her home, as
it always would be.

Once, the house was her treasure, only recently, did it run down, not because of her unwillingness, sickness, drove her away, regrettably, she had to let it go.

Much later, I moved the stove, underneath, lay two crisp hundred-dollar bills, as if she seemed to be say, "I'm sorry, I had to leave, please take care of my little house," and I did.

The Storm

The air is hot and steamy, something is
About to happen, leaves curl upward toward the
Sky, birds call endlessly for everyone
To listen, a cool breeze blows, the smell of
Rain is in the air, trees become as still
As death, an ominous foreboding is
In the wind, fear of the unknown has enveloped
Everything in its path.

The sky turns black as the darkest night, the
Wind changes direction, strong gusts blow, the
Temperature plummets, trees bending, intermittent
Raindrops explode hitting the ground, the wind
Grows louder with each blow.

The wind is roaring, tree branches bending,
Breaking, ice pellets pelt everything, turning
The ground white, sirens can be heard in the
Distance, the day has become night.

Clouds are raging, growing, moving fast,
Rain is coming down in sheets saturating
The ground, puddles turn to rivers running
Toward the sewers, filling, the river is rising,
Moving fast, growing, overflowing their banks.

The sidewalks are covered
With falling debris, a break in the clouds
Can be seen, the sun shows traces of a
Glimmer of hope, a ray of sunshine peeks
Through the clouds, and the storm has moved on.

Tending the Garden

Working the ground, the feel
of warmth on my back, a
breeze cools my brow, each spade full
brings the image to reality,
a plot of ground into a garden.

One shovel then two,
each broken up by a hoe, blisters
form on my hands, earth worms awakened,
today, nothing sleeps, all must
leave to survive.

Rows are marked with string, seed packages
opened, one by one they enter the ground,
covered with dirt,
watered,
precisely,
not to crowd, not to over water, remove
the unwanted plants, weeds, up to no
good, watch and then and only then
will it grow.

Each day, the weeds are pulled,
plants watered, cultivated and
fertilized,
watching,
waiting,
anticipating,
with luck the plants produce
a tomato, a cucumber, a bean.

Clouds form, rain, maybe something
more sinister,
wind,
hail,
the garden destroyers, I pray for rain,
the bean leaves have been eaten,
pesticide, maybe, maybe not.

Stormy Day

A dark gloomy scene
fills my window pane,
a cool breeze blows,
suggesting rain.

Out of the west,
flashes burst, lighting
the sky, night verses day,
seconds pass, rumbling,
oh so far away.

Closer now, howling,
trees bending, breaking,
light smashing, struggling
to be heard, rain boring
down on all of us
this stormy day.

Shortly, the sun
breaks through,
the rain moves away,
leaving, only red, yellow,
green and blue.

Slot Fever

Cha-Ching
Cha-Ching
Cha-Ching
The moneys drop in.

Spinning
Spinning
Spinning
All with a single pull.

Triple Bars
Double Bars
Single Bars
Flickering past the window.

Slowly
Slowly
Slowly
Reels predict a winner.

Cha-Ching

Cha-Ching

One less

Than when you started.

Cha-Ching

Cha-Ching

Cha-Ching

Again, the money drops in.

Spinning

Flashing

Sevens

Come by.

Spinning

Flashing

Bars

Come by.

Slowly
Slowly
Slowly
Nothing.

Cha-Ching
Cha-Ching
Cha-Ching
Again, in goes the money.

Spinning
Spinning
Slowly, slowly
Again, nothing.

Cha-Ching, Cha-Ching, Cha-Ching
Again the money drops in
Spinning slowly, slowly
All single bars.

Ha-Ha

Ha-Ha

Ha-Ha

I'm only down a thousand.

Loved From Afar

The time was not right,
is it ever, you had
your life, I had mine,
infatuation, maybe, maybe love.

Remembering, we had something,
something very special, though
we dare not act on it, for we
feared reprisal.

The first time I saw you,
I did not know of my
infatuation, that would
come much later.

Our friendship grew, the image
of you made my blood boil,
your aroma quickened my heart,

the curve of your neck filled me
with desire.

I knew you felt it, the touch of
your hand when you came near,
the graze of a hip, the warmth
of your smile.

Spending hours together, when
we could be elsewhere, collecting
images for what would have to sustain
us when we parted, longing to be
together again.

Our ritual continued for
months, never acting, friendship
growing, until that fateful
parting.

Many years latter, I knew
we had given up something

special, a shared moment,
we had loved, loved from afar.

Blue Skies

Bonded by fate,
we rallied, for something better.
How small, we were alone,
together, we have made a difference.
Blue Skies.

Floating above,
the blueness made us one,
members of a force,
larger, than ourselves.
Blue Skies.

Time moves forward,
never changing, our hearts,
one in mind, body and spirit.
A team.
Blue Skies.

Now, we go, our separate ways,
only linked, by the time,
we spent together,
as a team.
Forever.
Blue Skies.

The Reason I Live

I've been captivated
by water, raging forcefully
in my mind, it's marked me
early in life, I remember running
in the rain, sitting in puddles.

Never can I pass a
body of water without gazing,
questioning, where does it's
beauty comes from, sometimes I even
wade, feeling the current run through my legs.

I always stop to gaze,
at the rivers mighty current,
ripples on the surface
catch my eye, as it navigates
a rock, a log, forcing away any object.

Many times, in my youth,
I have dreamed of taking a trip, from
the beginning of a river to it's end,
maybe I must take the time, for this
is the reason I live.

Together, Again

Today,
I sit, trying
to come up with
something unique,
my own, family
tradition,
one that circumvents
time and space,
to bring us together
when we are apart.

All,
I can
think of,
is in the
"Stars".

Today,

I sit, under
God's bright lights,
frozen, knowing,
that my family
and friends,
somewhere, anytime,
could look up
at the sky
and we would be
together, again.

The Painting

The hill stands above
the water's shore glimmering, held
confined by tall green pine trees.

Houses line the waters edge, a dock
protrudes into a bay, protected by a
sliver of land, extending into the lake.

A duck sits on the water of the bay, boats
appear motionless except for a white frothy wake,
a sailboats billowy sail suggest movement.

An eagle is suspended in the
sky, like a child's mobile hanging
above a crib, clouds seem frozen in time.

The bend of the trees, signal wind, dark
tones become shadows, light tones become sun
shine, trees are mirrored at the waters edge.

Just for an instant, we are able to capture a moment in time, the lake is etched in our minds, it becomes the picture, the painting.

Growing Old

He used to glide,
as he walked,
effortlessly,

Now, he stumbles,
wincing with each
step, each stride.

Aches, have entered
his joints, his bones,
shaking, unsteady,

He has lost, life's
excitement and
is growing old.

Today I Start a Journey

Today, I start a journey,
somewhere between birth and
death,

Sitting, analyzing, wondering,
what makes a man
remembered?

Is it, his frailty,
his pride or just his
naivete?

Today, I remove the worn
planks of decking, exchanging them, for
concrete,

For those I have touched, have I given them
a strength or a weakness, to be ground away by
time?

The Distraction

In the dark, walking, stumbling
toward the scraps of wood,
stacked in the fire pit.

Boys at my heels, like baby
porpoises, huddling together, in
shark infested waters.

Outcasts? No, uneasy about
their Grandmother's fate
and what lies ahead.

Uncle B's driving the tractor, pulling
a wagonload of campers,
toward the fire pit.

Arriving, via
the Bonfire
Express.

Quickly, lighting the fire,
whoosh, up goes the human
effigy, Guy Faulks.

Standing, thinking,
wondering, why death
has to be so cruel.

Rosy runs up shouting,
Will you play ball
with me?

Kneeling, grabbing her
around the waist,
standing.

Lifting her, throwing
her, up into the air, as
if, she were a ball.

Immediately, my anxiety,
seems to have gone flying
out into space.

Catching her, hugging her, Rosy's
face, is as white as
the ball, she is carrying.

Not with me,
she says,
I'm not the ball.

Setting her down, holding her,
so she
would not fall.

Releasing her, she still
stumbles, hurrying to get
away.

Running as fast as
her, little legs would take her,
"Mommy", she yells.

On the way back to Mom's side, realizing, a little girl had touched me, making me see Mom's immanent death from a different view.

Not alone, anymore, in my sorrow, the world
still had alot to offer me,
Thank you Rosy.

Losing My Convictions

I travel this
world, trying to hang on
to my convictions,
holding on with all
my will.

slowly they fade, lost
with my youth,
lost with my values,
wondering, if I have lost my
soul, also.

How Did This Happen?

That fateful day in
September, fear surfaced
For a nation, once again.

I woke to the telephone,
"Turn on the TV",
A voice said to me.

Passenger planes flew into
Buildings, those images
Played over and over.

Another plane, hit
Another building, crashing,
Emitting fire everywhere.

Fire burning, smoke billowing,
People running, jumping, suddenly,
Crashing, down came the building.

Suddenly, it was apparent,
The second building was
Going to come down, also.

For an instant,
Everyone felt the sorrow,
For the brave, for the unfortunate.

That September day, calm was
No more, all planes had stopped
Flying, diverted elsewhere.

Walking outside, so clear, so
Quiet, too still, fear
Was settling in.

A nation, shocked
By the tragedy, slowly
They would recover.

Mourning collectively,
A nation brought together,
For a short time.

Today, still recovering
From that day in September, when
Everything stopped, for a brief moment.

A nation was unprepared,
And still no one knows,
"How did this happen"?

Columbia, where are you?

Today, the world stopped,
for a few brave men and women,
while searching, for answers to
questions, once thought to be in
the heavens, much like the tower
of Babbel, they came crashing down.

Their remains spread, everywhere,
the message always seems to be the same,
as explorers, we have become too
passive, too comfortable,
slow down, become more meticulous,
for life is oh so precious.

We need to be sure, is the loss
of one life worth the exploration,
worth the conquest, maybe the answer
lies, in each of us, are we willing,
to make the sacrifices ourselves,
for the good of others?

Danny's Sign of Spring moved me so
(For Linda)

Today, I read
that which
was
written long ago, it
moved me so, I felt
I had to write
this for
you.

What I read
made me
think
of my lost youth
and many springs
which had meant
so much to
me.

Today, I write with
that same
intensity,
to build, to
grow, convictions
for those
without
any.

My Secret Place

Deep within my mind lies
a very special place,
nobody's allowed, but me,

always alone, saying
nothing, yet surreal,
calmly, I am transformed,

concentrating, I allow
my mind to wander,
transfixed on nothing,

I hear the rhythmic beating
of my heart, nothing
else seems to matter,

once there, my mind is able
to capture an
idea, so elusive, so

far reaching, so pure, maybe
just for a moment,
original thought,

they come as poetry,
vivid words, splashing on
the canvases of my mind,

my pen, is the receptor
gathering thoughts,
storing them on paper, so

calm, so quiet, peace fills
my soul, soothing me, like
waves lapping at the shore,

I say the words aloud
for they sing my message,
encoded for the cynics,

anything invading my thoughts,
is foreign to my
work, unwelcome,

no one can enter unless
I give in, that will
never happen for

hidden, deep within my mind
there lies a very
special place, my secret place.

Star Lake

Walking upward, toward the sky,
ever so slowly, I ascended the hill,
below, lie the most beautiful vision
I have ever gazed upon, a lake.

It's blue water glistening, sun rays
transforming a hue of the bluest of blues,
blending into the azure of the sky,
broken only by the lime green of the
tree line, north woods pines.

A warm breeze blows,
scurrying over the grass covering the hill,
bending the golden wheat, breaking, reflections
of the sun as it crosses the silent surface
of the lake, it's contour, appearing
to go on forever.

Many times, I have sat there,
gazing over the dark gray water, it's

churning white caps, raging, from being
mistreated, trees swaying, watching the pelting
rain as it crosses the bay, the sun's warmth lost
in battle with the cold of a passing cloud,
darkness descends, allowing the stars
to touch the waters of the lake.

With daylight, humming birds ascend,
flying sorties, attacking feeders, frenzied
abandonment, Loons calling, continuously,
a message of love, Eagles perching, high over head,
watching over the bay, shoulder to shoulder,
Chipmunks scurrying, mouths full, Otters playing
in the shallow water of the Islands.

With night comes large predator fish,
patrolling the waters, searching, for unwitting
victims, Star Lake, it's beauty, constantly,
reminding me of a humility, pulling me,
back, time after time,
year after year.

My Last Moments at the Lake

Standing, gazing,
trying to take in
the lakes beauty,
one last time.

The autumn wind blows,
cold and crisp,
chilling me enough
to put on gloves.

A loon dives
deep in the bay
where the dock used to sit,
natures way of saying, Goodbye.

I stood alone, a special moment,
just me and the lake,
not a sound could be heard,
remembering.

Red, brown, orange foliage,
the vistas of fall, fill
my senses, as I stare
across the bay, wondering.

Soon the bay
would be covered
with ice and
I would not see it.

Where has the time gone,
would I ever be so happy
as I was at the lake,
life can be so very cruel.

With Spring, the ice would thaw,
the wild life
would return and
I would not see it.

The others say Goodbye
in their own special way,
some get angry, some take a
walk or even a boat ride.

I enter the van,
pulling away from the lake,
a tear runs down my cheek, for
the lake is gone, forever.

Alone

Sometimes,
I just want
to scream out
as loud as
I can, running
away as fast as
my old legs
will carry
me.

I want
to be set free,
away from everyone,
so no one
would ever care,
what happened to
me.

As if
anyone would,
for someone to
care, they must
connect,
no one does,
anymore.

My Neurosis

I struggle
through
each day,
with thoughts,
of needful
tasks,
not hard,
many very
simple.

Each
moment,
the size
of the task
grows, always
getting larger.

My mind has to take time
to find faults, to battle,
to foresee all possible scenarios,
just to be prepared.

The project eventually becomes
too big, no one could possibly
finish it, not in this
life time or any other.

Those ideas invade my mind, tiring me,
forcing me to quit, never to
have started a small task,
tonight, the garbage will not go out.

I wonder where

I wonder where
my sanity
has gone?

My thoughts, wander,
jumbled together,
flighty and sad.

I wonder where
I'll ever land?

If ever, I
feel, it won't be
be very pretty.

Crashed, Smashed,
to wonder, why,

I wonder where
my sanity
has gone?

Foot Steps Echo in the Night

Each day, he walks to earn his money,
walks just to keep afloat, each night
he walks to feed his family,
spending, just a few pennies,

shadows lurk behind each light post,
foot steps echo in the night,
and still, he trudges on.

Each day, he stops to purchase
a morsel, stops to feed his family,
each night he won't allow them
to go to sleep hungry,

shadows lurk behind each light post,
foot steps echo in the night,
and still, he trudges on.

Each evening, he leaves for home,
leaves for his family, each night,
a stranger points a gun, "Friend,
your money or your life"

shadows lurk behind each light post,
foot steps echo in the night,
and still, he trudges on.

Each day, he hands over his earned
money, hands it all away, everytime,
they ask him "why?", and he answers,
"I must feed my family."

shadows lurk behind each light post,
foot steps echo in the night,
and still, he trudges on.

A Taste of Freedom

(For Jordan)

Soaring, through the
clouds, I lost track of
time.

How many get the
chance to soar as an
Eagle?

Commercial travel
does nothing to provoke
thought,

to stimulate the
senses, to live a fuller
life.

The mere idea
of gliding over
pastures,

high above rivers, full of rushing
rapids, houses hiding people, excites me
beyond possibility.

From the cockpit, the crowds look like
swarms of insects, preparing for the
winter.

Cars, crawl toward
destinations, nothing seems real,
anymore.

How can it be?

Passing through a
cloud, I dream of another
time,

a time of freedom, while sailing through the heavens.

Now, I depend on others to enjoy my freedom, it comes at a price, not controlled by me.

The Canyon of My Youth

The canyon lies beneath,
like a grand lady, waiting,
crevices line my eyesight,
teetering rocks hang precariously
over the vastness of the canyon,
a slight vibration could be my end,
the Colorado hugs the walls,
twisting its way along the floor,
grays, yellows, browns, greens,
hidden below the azure sky,
vibrant rose streaks emit
from the sun, as it sinks
into the horizon,
a foggy mist creeps into the
depths of the canyon walls,
as osprey glide high over the
rock formations, occasionally,
sinking into its depths,

Bright Angel Lodge sits, reminding
me of several days of my youth,
of a donkey, an author
and together their story,
befriended me, one lonely summer,
now, the lodge sits,
merely to house
visitors, for the night.

The Special People

(for Chris)

We belong to many different groups,
of all shapes, races, religions, sexes,
the handicapped, those afflicted, those
unlucky for they were chosen.

I never know when I
will meet someone special,
never taking the time to learn
their names and I should.

They are the meek, the mild,
who have been said, will inherit the
earth, only they were dealt a poor hand,
now struggling to endure.

A higher power has thrown them a curve,
knowing they can handle the added
burden, they are our inspirations,
our role models.

If only we know what they know? They
rise, each day to overcome huge obstacles,
which we can not even comprehend,
they are the special people.

Gone Forever

Walking, slowly
through the yard,
broken, rusted objects
line the driveway, far
as I can see.

It seems, I've entered a graveyard,
where old things die,
items that once brought
so much joy, now
they are but junk.

Growing sad, I realize,
someone's dreams lie there
in the ruins, rotting, waiting
to be revived, like
a phoenix, to live again.

Most are not reborn,
they are gone,
gone forever and
so are the
dreams.

A Chill

fills my senses
browns, oranges, yellows
meld into the sky, a
back drop for this
autumn day.

Released,
a leaf tumbles,
slowly
falling, slowly
rotating.

Caught by a breeze,
the rusty fingers
slithering from
tree to tree, branch
to branch.

Floating, plummeting
toward the ground,
it's blanket of
velvet leaves, maples,
walnuts, and birches.

Winds catch the oaken
fingers sending them skyward,
rolling them slightly,
across the street,
over the creek.

Swirling them,
toward the surface of the water,
touching, capturing, sending
them far away,
forever.

My Way

I have

lived

a

good life,

do not

cry, do not

mourn my

loss,

remember

me, for

I have

lived my

life,

my way.

My World

A small sphere, sitting
in my hand, slowly
caressing it's surface,
the earth is mine, to
do as I wish.

Hand held flat, it rolls
to the center, now
sitting alone, so small,
I realize, I
am in control.

With my thoughts, shaping
my destiny, I
reach out, together, we
can change the
world.

The Major

Recently, someone asked me,
why I rejoined Kiwanis?

The first time, I hoped
to sell a computer,

you see, I was asked to speak
at a club in Illinois, it was 1983,

I thought I was to demonstrate a machine,
I had no idea, they were looking for me,

everyone reached out, in friendship and
together, we helped to build a better community,

every club has someone, that was the Major,
a stickler, for procedures,

a mere grunt, in Nam, where he drank a quart each night,
never did I know the baggage, he had to carry,

an insurance man, major in the reserves,
he disarmed bombs, my friend the over achiever,

in college, he became a Kiwanian,
president of our club and lieutenant governor,

together, we built a shelter, for the handicapped,
he was my friend, my mentor, a model of who I am,

my proudest moment, playing Santa, for the
underprivileged, now that's another story,

work became too much, I had to quit, many years
later, I heard my friend died by his own 45,

now, you ask me, why, I joined again? For my friend,
for you Pat, I will never forget.

I Remember

that day, as if
it were yesterday,
the day was cool and oh so cloudy,
there he laid, never moving,
never responding to my queries,
not answering, not adding a thing.

His eyes
were black as coal,
as I looked deep within,
I saw his soul
and I knew,
it was over.

That day I would remember
forever, the day I knew
he had quit, quit trying,
quit wanting to live,
for me, that day
he had died. I cried.

Canada

Driving north, we travel,
sixteen boring hours, reflection time,
anticipation grows,
we read, play cards and become friends,
at least for the next week,
on the way we stop, for gas,
food and change drivers,
everyone gets a chance,
onward to International Falls,
breakfast and the Canadian Border. **We go on.**

At the border checkpoint,
a guard asks a flurry of questions,
nervously, we answer,
awaiting, anxiously,
the nod to continue,
his decision, ahead or off to the side,
which is to be our destiny, today,

ahead it is, we pay the toll,
continuing to Sioux Narrows,
Kenora, and the docks. **We go on.**

Arriving in Kenora,
everything is weighed,
loaded, amongst the mightiest plane,
taxiing over the water,
up, up into the air we soar,
with a mighty roar, no one can hear,
flying high,
below water lay, rocks and trees,
everywhere, as far as we can see,
the blue water merges into the horizon,
rocky shores blend, into the lake's contour,
rocks bobbing, in a sea of shimmering sunrays,
reflecting off the mirror of ripples and
into the sky for all to see. **We go on.**

Seagulls fly, from Island to Island,
searching for scraps,

eagles perch, keeping the peace,
Bull Moose trample the forests,
crashing through anything in their paths,
bears sauntering for food,
wherever an easy meal can be found. **We go on.**

The plane circles the outpost,
landing with a whoosh on the water,
taxiing to the crowded pier,
people line the dock,
anticipating a flight home,
off the plane, we climb,
replacing the oppressed,
quickly the prisoners board,
the only means off the island,
away from the dock, the transport crawls,
again, off with a full load,
people, gear and garbage,
revving the engine the plane jerks forward,
over the water they go,
up, up into the sky,

just seconds before crashing into the trees,
serenity has been restored, once more. **We go on.**

Now, we are the imprisoned,
shackled for at least a week,
quickly, busying ourselves,
examining everything,
the kitchen, the outhouse, searching,
the icehouse, the fish cleaning house,
gas and garbage cans and more,
new boats, new motors,
nothing left to chance. **We go on.**

We quickly clean and unpack,
releasing our sleeping bags in our bunks,
unloading the food, away,
into the cabinets, refrigerator,
go our supplies, again
loading our fishing gear into the boats,
I yell, we go to find to fish,
check the plugs, we don't want to sink,

check the gas, we must get back,
gear into the boats,
we go, away now, away,
adrenaline is pumping,
now on a mission to forget
where we came from,
to catch the first walleye,
northern or maybe even a bass. ***We go on.***

Back trolling with jigs,
we cast with lures,
to catch a fish,
our excitement is at its peek,
for today we fish,
some have waited their whole lives
for this moment and now we are here,
in Canada, fishing. ***We go on.***

His Day

(For Walter)

Today,
he enters the trench,
somewhere in France,
Cantigny, Marne, Argonne.

No mans land sprawls out in front of him,
separating the two sides,
overhead flashes brightening the sky,
whistles blowing, the offensive has started.

Bombs exploding over his head,
machine guns spraying out in front of him,
outlines of dark, gloomy shadows, pepper the
battlefield, so young, so dead.

He scans the land from a trench,
a periscope to see all without dying,

everything lay rotting, the hopes, the dreams, no more.

Gas masks hang, alone, unused,
wounded lie in their bunks, too hurt to move,
death is all around and the reinforcements do not come.

Today, he prepares himself to man the gun,
prepares himself to die, five have tried, before him, five have died, before him, now it's his turn.

He will try to turn back the enemy,
he will die trying, as the others had,
still he does his duty, like the five before him and still he dies.

Today we travel a familiar path,

not a secret, that it has been traveled many times before,

Never has the outcome of war, favored man, never has the world,
had a better reason to come together as one,

War has always had a following,
only after many die, is the price too high,

Today, I realize man's unwillingness
to love others, as ourselves,

I compel you, we must come together, for no nation
can be, more righteous than another,

No mere man, can change the course, once it starts,
only together, can we change the world,

Peace begins with a small act of kindness,

and love keeps it growing,

Today, we are traveling a path,
very close to destruction,

Mere bystanders, we watch, hoping, someone will
stop the insanity, but it never comes,

We wait, for someone, today, it's our
turn, lets stop a war,

It doesn't matter why the dove has
died, for it's still dead,

death is forever and nothing we do, will
ever bring the dove back.

Peace onto you,
God Bless Everyone.

Graduation Day

A day in May, 2003 was one of pride, for me. It was a day like any other day, raining I think, although for you, the sun was shining as always. A breeze blew a strand of long dark hair into your eyes momentarily, grasping the lock, you tucked it behind your ear as always. Today was your special day, one of those few we're allowed, Graduation Day.

I wasn't able to be there, but in spirit, I walked with you. Ten years before, was my day. It only took a mere seventeen years for me and when I finished, I felt empty, sorry it was over. For me, the pursuit was more rewarding than the goal. The years have changed me, I have developed a deep seated pride, for I over came the odds and won, just like you. Be proud Katie, as we are of you.

Once, I looked to you as my own and today, we're not able to be as close as we once were. Still, I remember seeing you for the first time, through the sparkling glass, you were lying with the others, so small, so beautiful, your mother's smile beaming like sunshine.

Over the years, we saw how gifted you were, always striving to be the best, never excepting second place, never quitting, even after hitting an occasional bump in the road. You never quit.

Today, Katie, let me give you but a wisp of my wisdom. Always follow your own inner voice and you will be happy. You'll make mistakes, but do not fear them, for they will make you into the person your supposed to be. Mistakes are successes of a wrong time, a wrong place, keep striving, reaching and you will grow.

FOR I AM AN AMERICAN

I am an American,
without any
doubt,

my values are solid,
my convictions without
reproach,

I listen
for the words of
others,

weighing the message, it's
meaning, only then, will I make up my
mind,

I fight for my ideals,
I fight to be
heard,

many have died, to give
me my voice, for them, I
am thankful,

I'll disagree with
policy, write letters,
march,

freedoms, are not mine
unless I'm willing to
fight,

first by diplomacy,
lastly by force, for
I AM AN AMERICAN.

The Righteous War

Today, war entered my life,
the first time I saw
the political side,

many believe in
righteousness, hidden, buried
beneath, a selfish role,

through a view of a few,
still the majority rallies
with the troops,

ever wonder
who rallies for the
dead,

who feels for them,
for they
feel, no more,

what
makes dying
right?

Only Suffering

War started today,
our missiles banged
into Baghdad,
disappointment has crept
into my thoughts,
for my country
started the war.

We watched as
if we were innocent,
viewing scenes of death and
dying, strategies were
discussed as in sport,
all are guilty, like
the nazi's, for not saying
no, for not protesting.

Each action will
be recorded, remembered,
discussed, so it will
never happen again, but
it will, it always does,
I wonder, who will be
remembered as being
right, no one yet knows.

I am saddened,
saddened that we forgot,
that war is hell and death
is forever, that prisoners
are tortured and war
never brings peace,
only suffering.

War is still War

Remember,
the summer, Billy tormented the
neighborhood, the strongest arm
always prevails.

Understand,
dominance, a ruling monarch,
not for bravery, but inciting fear, eventually,
all dictators are over thrown.

Finally,
Mark stood up against him, a few
words, four stitches and Billy was
still in control.

Someone,
killed Marks baby ducks,
drowned, everyone

blamed Billy.

That day,
the neighborhood went to war,
sides drawn, everyone eager
for a fight.

Freedom
was their chant, the day was
oh so chilly, the day
we met Billy.

No one
knew, who killed the ducks,
no one cared, for the mighty
Billy was no more.

Everlasting Peace

Today,

I travel

back in time,

with every

intention

to understand why,

who do I

have to

thank

for War.

Rigid

policies

spring forth

fear, marches

formed from differences

appear,

soldiers fight

then die,

for just a noble gesture.

Oh

the pain,

force always

begets force,

fear, never

a means to

an end

and death is

forever.

Causes

are not more

than life,

suffering

must stop,

discussion

has to continue,

war spawns only

war and Peace may
bring about
Everlasting Peace.

Fail them, not

Fail them, not for the
American Dream has been
mashed,
smashed,
masked
to hide the truth,
the end justifies any means.

Fail them, not for we do not see,
the goals seem to change with the
tick,
tock,
of the clock,
our support has always been righteous,
for we do not take war lightly.

Fail them, not for we vow
to defend with our lives,

liberty,

freedom,

our way of life,

but not by aggression, till now

skewed by greed, power, oh yes, oil.

Fail them, not for everyone in America is

not blind, does not believe the war is right,

for death is forever,

soldiers die giving us

a voice,

I would fail them, not

to use it.

The Plant

Constant murmur,
drowning the chatter
of the children, splashing
in the pool.

Birds chirping
foretelling
of the extended
heat.

An Airplane soaring
overhead, only it's
roar of its engines
tells me of its presence.

Not sweltering,
just hot, bordering
miserable,
humid enough to sweat.

Still the motor
can be heard
in the
distance.

An occasional bug
dive bombs, annoying me
enough to write
about him.

The morning dove hoots,
a robin sings,
announcing
evening has come.

Still the
hum,
radiates
the ear.

If I wasn't
distracted, the constant
racket would become
deafening.

Slowly, I would focus
on it, it alone,
driving me, driving me
crazy.

This Cage We Call Life

Where are the
people? Where did
they go?

Those who
love with all
their heart.

Having chosen love
over everything
else.

Knowingly, searching
forever, never
wanting anything more.

Each of us, finding love,
is transformed into who
we are, forever.

Our lives magnified
superimposed in our minds
eye, as if we live in a dream.

How can love
be so
great?

Struggling alone,
together, we become
one.

Somehow, we choose life
over death and a child is born,
our child.

The light of the world
has shined on us for a
special moment.

We pray, thanking the Lord
or whoever gave us
this miracle.

If only it would last,
there are no
guarantees.

Life is not so
simple, nor
is love.

Special memories are lost with
the images of the day,
cluttering our minds with trash.

Our love is buried
in a heap of failures,
burdens and stress.

Somewhere we
forget, forget
to love.

The light dims,
left long enough,
it goes out, forever.

Now we are again alone,
wondering what
went wrong?

Struggling each
day, feeling
oh, so alone.

Our lives have little
meaning, for true love has
escaped our grasp.

As a butterfly, love has flown away or died in this cage we call life.

By Beginning

The inch-worm
knows it, he never
had to learn it.

Butterflies
develop it, to use flying
long distances.

Salmon
swim for it, never
do they tire.

Animals
of every type let it,
become there only desire.

Every Species
knows it's done, but
never knowing how.

Inventions, Exploration, Humanization, all were born because of it.

Compassion, Understanding, Education, nothing comes without a price.

Together, we succeed, just simply by beginning.

What is Fiction

They say I don't read fiction,
it's not the truth,

Is it because the plot
couldn't resemble a neighbor's life,

Is it the not so real characters,
who are modeled after Uncle Pete or Aunt Rose,

Is it a made up town which reminds
you of Minneapolis or St. Pete,

Is it a back story that could have
happened to you as a kid,

Is it a supporting character that might have been
Miss Smith, your first grade teacher,

Maybe the gas station could be the

one down the street,

What is fiction, but the scenes many of us have seen everyday of our lives.

The Writing Stopped

My pen
slips, turning
back in, causing
me to stop writing,
accidentally, killing
my creative flow,
for a moment.

    The enjoyment
    stopped, when
    my pen ran
    dry.

My ideas
don't always
come, when
worries
crowd my
mind.

> The thoughts
> stopped, when
> my pen ran
> dry.

My pen
turns down
again,
killing
a day,
a month,
a year.

> The writing
> stopped, when
> my pen ran
> dry.

A Pencil Poised

A pencil poised
waiting for a
thought that
might not come,

still my hand
is ready to
capture a brief
whim of an idea,

anything,
to start the
pen moving
again,

one word,
one line written,
forming a page,
a poem, a story.

My Ghost, the Writer

I move my pen across
the parchment, sometimes with
such precise strokes,
proceeding without
my guiding I wonder
if its really me,

my conscious mind appears
blank yet the other, does
not speak until I
sleep or so I thought,
I pick up a pen I
feel someone else is

in control, I write for
my mind is empty
though my pen dances
across the page, I

write outrageous words
of imagery thoughts

of emotion symbols
of happiness hidden
bits of my sorrow,
never used by me
before, maybe My Ghost,
the Writer, he knows.

A Poet

Today, he wakes,
looking in the mirror,
gazing on a countenance of a man,
a vision of a poet.

A man, a woman, a symbol, who
takes risks and writes the words,
capturing their most hidden
secrets, feelings that live
deep inside.

They view the words not as poetry,
although captured is the moment,
inspiration for an audience,
that may never come, inspiring
reflection and thought, to think, to live,
to believe in a better tomorrow.

Again, his feelings grow too large,
he begins to write, the words, spilling
onto the page, through the ink
of his pen, his thoughts come alive, once again.

Two Lives

I've been lucky to
have lived two lives,
one for money and the
other for me.

One life to subsist and
the other to contribute
a mere thought, maybe create
an idea that can take hold,
changing another's life forever.

Maybe the world needs us dreamers,
maybe we create hope for others,
maybe my ideals will strengthen the
worlds values, leading toward a more
righteous tomorrow, just maybe.

In one life I took orders, now I write of injustices and of utopia, what could be, hinting at what is, hoping it won't last, the righteous conflict and the resolution.

And just maybe, we will be more than just small players, maybe we will be active in making a contribution, making the world a better place.

Summer of my youth

My used shinny silver bike,
fenders glimmering, shimmering in the sun,
the book rack usually held my basketball,
the bike light never worked from day one,

I always cared for that bike,
it was a symbol of my freedom,
freedom from the house and the
four walls of my bedroom,

I remember those days as the wind blew
in our faces, we rode hard and furious
to our interlude with destiny and
the rest of our lives,

That first day was like any other,
hot and oh so muggy, a great
day to be fifteen and free

of all worldly burdens,

All that mattered to us,
was riding, riding like the wind,
past the open door of the factory,
where workers looked out and waved,

I remember hitting the loose gravel,
going down, falling and the pain, though
nothing would spoil our freedom,
we went on, bleeding all the way,

Across the railroad tracks, stopping
for a car, now, away we road, past the
cement company, to the fishing pier,
where we spent the summer of my youth.

A Portrait of a Man

Gazing, at my reflection in the mirror,
I see a stranger, he's staring back at me,
his hair is more gray than black,
the wrinkles are deeper, permanently,
scaring his face, where have the years gone,
the glimmer, has been replaced with a fog.

All I have, is the memories,
fading fast, long ago, images of
a career, a family, a dog.

My thoughts, a jumbled confused array of
disjointed bits of lost wit,
I was so quick at solving tasks, then this,
I speak, my words are lost, I utter a word,
then a pause, as I try to retrieve them all,
I just stare at the hole, getting bigger, in the wall,
wondering, why?

Be Proud, Jennifer

The air cools,

the leaves turn,

and fall,

downward,

as your

reign ebbs.

Remember,

those moments,

we came

together

as one,

to build, to serve.

Under your

watchful eye,

we rose,

to the challenge,

overcame our

failing numbers,

challenged by money woes
and still, we pulled
ourselves up, by
your side,
be proud, Jennifer,
for we are of you.

The Rodeo

Tonight at the Rodeo,
    Strangeness lurked everywhere.

Hats, boots, rain slickers, jeans,
    Cowboys walking with a limp.

Rope it, Ride it, Tie it, Break it.

Everyone came to the gate,
    Cowboys roping steers running to their mate.

Men climbed on wild horses for a ride,
    Were thrown from bulls of humongus size.

Bucking, bouncing, flying, breaking.

Cowboys, Clowns and pretty girls,
    They all came tonight to give it a whirl.

To prove themselves to their family and friends,
    To win the stakes and be crowned as the best.

Spring

Tulips
    Sway,
        In the breeze,
            Allowing their beauty to
                Infect our thoughts.

Birds
    Sing,
        To mates
            Now is the time
                To build their nests.

Turkeys
    Peck,
        At the ground, males
           Hold their feathers high,
                The mating ritual has begun.

Everything
    Senses,
        That spring has sprung,
            Everywhere trees budding, flowers
                Growing, insects flying.

Breezes
    Blow,
        into strong winds, the
            Rains begin and so does life,
                For spring has come.

Choices

Today,
    Tomorrow.
Night,
    Day.
Good,
    Evil.
On,
    Off.
Right,
    Wrong.
We make choices.

Positive or Negative
    Our choices are few,
        Our paths are many.

Where we go from here
    We call destiny.

Where we end up
>	We call life.

Birth,
>	Death,
>>	The beginning and the end
>>	Inbetween we make
>>>	Choices.

Thank You Son

(for Rob)

The phone rang at midnight,
never will I forget,
that moment.

Mom wouldn't make the mornings light,
the call, I expected and yet,
my knees went weak.

My stomach was churning,
I had to leave, immediately,
to be there, in time.

My son was with me,
still, I was in shock, childhood
memories burst in my head.

As I drove, miles streaked by,
the quiet seemed deafening,
evil dark lurked outside,

tears flowed with the solitude,
I spoke of memories, of youth,
and of mom.

That night, would be the
hardest of my life,
I remember, her fight,

her troubled breath, I prayed for
it to end, for her pain
to go, away.

By morning, she was gone,
I cried, a little, before
the realization made me crumble,

it was forever, and then
I wept, uncontrollably,
in the arms of my son.

Thank you son, for
being there.

My Choice

Today,

I must make a choice,

to help

someone

dear to me

or not.

It may

put me in a

precarious position,

but what doesn't?

Aren't we

supposed to help

those we can,

even if

it hurts?

Wouldn't
I want help
if I needed
it?

More
important is
my need
to help
because I can,

for nothing
is more satisfying
than being there
for family,
friends and another
human being,

especially,
someone that maybe
in need of
a hand.

Protesting War

"Man Arrested Protesting War",
    was the headline,
    or something,
the story didn't make
    the front page,

Protesters, marched,
    against the opening
    of a museum, a
display, vandalized,
    red paint thrown
    on the floor.

The famed Enola Gay,
    was on display,
the one that dropped
    the Atom bomb.

Then, I saw him,
nearly eighty years of age,
tears streamed down
his face, he was
the one, the vandal,

My thoughts would not stop,
obviously, of Asian descent,
his family or friends
might have been,

disintegrated, with not even a
body or fallen from
the fall out,

still the radiation, the pain,
war is hell and
I cried.

Outside My Window

Sitting at my keyboard, the day before Christmas, sleigh bells echo across the meadow, a horse trots in the distance, snow has begun falling outside my window, the ground has turned white and still it continues.

My shopping is finally done, still I have to wrap, the warmth of Christmas has entered my heart, as it has every year since I started to write, somewhere my thoughts have turned to peace, love and giving for that is truly me, the message I hold sacred deep, deep within my soul.

Outside my window the snowflakes have gotten bigger, the road is covered with an opaque sugar, my pine sits green against the white, the darkness has turned bright, an occasional car drives slowly, lights seen moving far off in the distance.

Time

Pen in hand
roller ball
and ink

Smoothly
rolling
upon my page

No longer
crossing
out

No longer
struggling
with my thoughts

Time
has given me
clarity

A
sense
of peace

Along
with

gray hair.

Life, A Game

Merely pawns,

black and white pieces,

Far, far away,

Selfish interests,

isolate,

One after

another,

Nothing remains,

Everything,

crashing down,

Falling,

Stopping,

Crushing,

Dying,

Checkmate.

The Last Story

Living in a time of
instant messages, each day,
the sound of the mail truck
brings me hurrying,
for someone might have written.

Each year, putting away,
my Christmas Cards,
each in it's own special folder,
cards, letters, folders seem empty,
few respond.

There wasn't time,
she always had a reason why,
still her file sits empty, maybe,
if only I had something, on those
oh so lonely days.

Each Christmas, I say it's
the last, the last story,
then a card moves me to write another,
desperately, yearning, for someone to
recognize my gift, for what it is.

Emotional Me

A tear rolls down my cheek,
they fog my eyes,
keep me from seeing
the good life has to offer,
emotional me.

I feel pain all around,
makes me wonder, if I'm
here to help others, to see,
what sits before them,
emotional me.

I write with them in mind
at least until I become
cold and hardened,
against the pain,
emotional me.

I try to fight the tears,
but I can't for too long,
they fog my eyes, choke my throat,
again, they roll down my cheeks,
emotional me.

About the Author

Dan Hanosh grew up in a small town in northern Illinois. A town where everyone knew each other and the reestablishing of values were always just one neighbor away. Growing up, parent-teacher conferences always had the same message for him, Dan's a good student, when he's not daydreaming. Spending half of his life working with computers, he found he was in the wrong career. One day, while caught in a sudden rain storm, he found writing, on a trout stream, of all places. Now, his world revolves around his family, books and his writing. His message for all, "Dreams are Yours to Share".

Printed in the United States
20264LVS00002B/103-111